Francis Poulenc

Un Joueur de flûte berce les ruines

for solo flute

With a foreword by Ransom Wilson

Chester Music

Un Joueur de flûte berce les ruines

In late 1997, whilst reading the school newspaper at Yale University (where I am Professor of Flute), I noticed a short article about an 'important' collection of music manuscripts that had recently arrived at the University's Beinecke Rare Book and Manuscript Library. The collection was formerly the property of Frederick R. Koch, a Yale graduate, who had assembled over the course of several years a group of manuscripts, mostly by French composers.

I immediately made an appointment to see what I could of this collection and was confronted with an immense catalogue. Its riches include manuscripts by Debussy, Ravel, Berlioz, Fauré, Gounod, Massenet, Duparc, Poulenc, Walton, Mozart, Schubert, Wagner, Puccini and Chopin, amongst many others. Indeed, in acquiring this collection, Yale University overnight became the location of the largest repository of French music manuscripts in North America, and probably the largest outside France.

One of the catalogue entries was highly puzzling: a work for solo flute by Francis Poulenc. Like most flute players, I had assumed that Poulenc had written no music for flute alone. I asked to see the manuscript, and was astonished to find the present work, written in Poulenc's own familiar hand.

The hitherto unknown *Un Joueur de flûte berce les ruines* ('A flute player lullabies the ruins') is dated 1942. The manuscript had apparently passed from its dedicatee, Madame Paul Vincent-Vallette, directly into the hands of a collector, and had eventually come into Frederick Koch's possession. The title seems to have been taken from the accompanying woodcut engraving, *Joueur de Flûte*, based on a sculpture in the Maison de l'Abbé Grécourt. Beyond that, though, almost no information about this little piece has yet come to light.

Un Joueur de flûte berce les ruines is in a modal, melancholic style. Its contours and economy recall the composer's earliest works, such as the *Mouvements perpétuels* (1918) and perhaps even some sections of the *Rapsodie nègre* (1917). I have performed it in concert in the United States, Canada, and France, and audiences are invariably enchanted with the piece. Short and simple, but of undeniable beauty, *Un Joueur de flûte berce les ruines* is undoubtedly an important addition to the solo flute repertoire.

Performance note: When playing this work in concert, I have found it effective to add a repeat sign (back to the beginning) before the final two bars, allowing the piece to be enjoyed twice.

RANSOM WILSON
New Haven, January 2000

UN JOUEUR DE FLUTE
BERCE LES RUINES

UN JOUEUR DE FLÛTE BERCE LES RUINES

FRANCIS POULENC

Origination by Barnes Music Engraving